IVAN ZHAVORONKOV

ZARATHUSTRA'S LARKMOTIF

Based on Anatoly Nazirov's
lyrical philosophical poem *Zarathustra*
Inspired by Friedrich Nietzsche's
Thus Spake Zarathustra

Edited by John Woodsworth

Toronto 2011

Zarathustra's Larkmotif. *Toronto 2011.*
By Ivan Zhavoronkov, Edited by John Woodsworth.
Copyright Translation © 2011 by Ivan Zhavoronkov.
All rights reserved. No part of this book may be used or
reproduced in any manner whatsoever without written
permission. Based on Anatoly Nazirov's lyrical philosophical
poem Zarathustra [Russian: *"Заратустра" (по мотивам*
произведения Ф. Ницше "Так говорил Заратустра".
Философская поэма. Санкт-Петербург – 1993)] inspired by
Friedrich Nietzsche's Thus Spake Zarathustra.

For more information on edition or to place an order,
please email at: zarathustra2001us@yahoo.com

ISBN: 978-0-9737762-3-2

Zarathustra's Larkmotif. 48 pages
Page format: 5.06" x 7.81"
Cover Design by Ivan Zhavoronkov
2011•Published by York University

Published by York University in Toronto.

Printed in Canada.

ZARATHUSTRA'S LARKMOTIF

Ivan Zhavoronkov. Zarathustra's Larkmotif

CONTENTS

ZARATHUSTRA IN THE VALLEY

As the morning star arises,
As the lark ascends in azure
And the lips of dawn glow brightly,
With her sharp eyes staring sternly
At the lakeside, down the mountain
There descends, rejuvenated,
Zarathustra toward the lakeside
He ten years ago abandoned.
As he sees the sightless forest,
And he hears the trail bewailing,
No resounding spirit's trodden
Verse's trailway for the ages:
Lines off metre, no more rhyming
In the land of verse forgotten:
Stanzas are no longer striking
But strike out right from the poem,
Strophes are not strict, but declining.
Gloom's glow-glances pierce the pondside.
Salty tear-slides blur his vision
Greeting that bright star's euphoria
With the tidings meant to flatter.
After melting gold with relish
In his mouth, for quite a decade,
Zarathustra is exhausted,

Waking golden-tongued in the morning.
Looking up toward the heavens,
Following the lark's ascending,
He beholds the gold orb's brightness,
"What would happen to your glory
If you had no one illumined?
Would you spread to me your flatt'ring
Golden parts, and do so daily,
If we did not increase our verses,
Putting wisest words together
Blank and unblank lines combining
In a mix of pride and wisdom?
Eagle-like, I reached the mountains,
Lark-like, rose from earth's confinements,
Serpent-like my thought ascended
From the honey and the poison
Of profound and misty wisdom.
With the clearest conscience ever,
I bring people brand new tidings,
But the world tide and the tidings
Are like tides untied inside me.
Like a snow-white melting iceberg
I am drawn toward you, mankind, now
By the reefs of raging billow,
By the rifts of shifting rhymings
With the rhythm of the spirit's
World of myths with pleas appealed to;
Wingèd nymphs drift me to verses.
I have come and have created
Lark-inspired odes of passion

To delight on earth the wisest
With their wholly silly folly,
And the poorest, to surprise them
With their secret, quiet riches.
I will bless you, star so tranquil,
If you evenly illumine
Me, the one who feels the greatest
Bliss of all upon the planet.
Into depths of all creation
I now pour myself for nations
From the cup of radiant temples
Of your blessed bliss and glory.
Full of golden heat, I hasten
Toward you, just as does the scarlet
Cow of dawn streaming with rosy
Milk — the light of splendid daybreak —
Trickling down through wispy, smoking
Clouds of flaming fire in heaven."

***

Scorched with thoughts, despair-afflicted,
Down the mount went Zarathustra,
Wandering into waning woodlands,
Drifting up in thought to mountains,
On a skylark's wings ascending;
Met an elder in the valley,
Who had left his holy cabin,
Seeking roots in rooted places,
Undecaying and unrotten.

With his eyes he quickly captured
Zarathustra walking briskly.
Breaking his devoted seeking,
He picked up a thought for thinking,
Scanned its root with vivid vision,
"Zarathustra, I recall you
By your eyes, the fires, remembered
By their shooting fiery sparkles
Flying star-like through the heavens,
Skylark's rise illuminating.
To the mountain you removed then
Your incinerated ashes,
Now your spirit's fire you carry
Fearlessly into the valley.
Don't you fear at all, pray tell me,
To be punished like all mortals
As an arsonist, a culprit,
By unkindly humankindness?
With your eyes as pure as children's
One could well comb the dishevelled,
Shuffled locks of careless people
Unawakened from their slumber.
Wake them not, they do not want it.
Your reward for trying to give them
Too much happiness will kill you.
What is more — you'll be considered
As an enemy thereafter.
Can't help dying if you love them.
I abandoned them forever,
For I loved them more than ever,

More than just my own existence.
Now my love to God is tendered.
Do not make them all-too-happy
Lest they think you greedy, thieving.
Throw the poor some alms and quickly
Get you hence, lest in departing,
You should breathe their rotten odour,"
Spoke the saint, a man of wisdom,
Left, with lagging steps retreating,
Songs surrounding him, escorting
Just like earthly gods now floating
Off with him in the far distance.
In the elder's wake, then, pondered
Zarathustra, twice not thinking,
"Yet I am not so poor and needy
To give paltry alms to people.
In these back woods not a single
Herald has been loudly crying,
Lark has never sung his roundelay —
This poor elder does not know that
God in heaven is no more dying.
But all gods died long ago."

                    ***

Zarathustra wandered onward
To a city on the foothills,
Where a multitude of rabble
In the market place swarmed dully.
Sad and tight, a tightrope dancer

11

Who had grieved all his existence
For the crowd began performing,
To the ground abruptly soaring,
To appear amid their laughter,
Shattered, battered, broken, dying,
Still a creature yet most worthless.
There resounded these discourses —
Zarathustra's mouth had dropped them:
"Humankind's existence's doubtful,
For the human who is destined
To be nothing but a monkey,
Is in fact a dirty river,
Overfull of imperfection.
Would the sea be quite sufficient
As to cleanse a human being
That is doomed too soon to perish?
Like a tightrope he is stretching
Over an abysmal chasm
And could easily there vanish.
I disdain the good existence,
For it makes me feel disgusted.
And your lofty life-vocation
Is a thoughtful refutation
On the part of bitter ages
With their ageing contemplations.
How I love all those aspiring
To destroy themselves in deepness —
Thus their hearts burn, in consumption.
For I love them all for falling
In profound, deep desolation

Where from depths of blackest darkness,
Taking wing to heaven's azure,
Rising upward like the skylark,
One can find one's own salvation.
For my virtue is a-striving
For such worthy degradation,
Showing sparks of strife and battle,
Strife with mankind's adumbration."

***

Molten lava, his discourses
Overflowed in high eruption,
Flowing downward as a river
Into frost-cold lakeside waters,
Feed for fish, in hungry places.
Crowd, within themselves withdrawing,
Fish becoming in the silence,
In response to his discourses
Blinking with their eyes wide-open,
Scattered soon, dispersing, like the
Motley dust in all directions.
Zarathustra, now abandoned,
Yet attended by his skylark,
Lovingly in his heart he pondered:

***

Just a little bit more foolish
Than a local fool amongst them,
Frank and candid and outspoken,
Did I look to them this noontide,
It would have as always added
To their pleasure to call any
Wisdom nothing but a folly.
I have been, therefore, entrusted
With the corpse, the last trustworthy,
Of the pitiful, despisèd —
Who, like crazy, strive with vigour
Once again, to own existence
Though endangering their wicked
Present life's existence, rising
Over death's abyss to plummet.
What a catch today! — no breathing,
Living soul, and I have gained the
Deadest body in the bargain.
Never mind, my friend, most worthy,
Poor and miserably wretched
Was your soul; it floated deader
Than your valiant, noble body
Broken by your soul, disloyal.
I intend myself to bury
You, as is your own intention
Deep within, your soul to bury
Deep within your own dead body —
Skylark be our own good witness.

***

Trail-worn-out, the weary traveller
Trod along, with his companion's
Baggy body on his shoulders.
When the grave gravediggers met him,
They remarked the corpse he carried
Was a dog dead as a dodo.
They advised that Zarathustra
Leave the town, and quickly, saying
That it was his own good fortune
That he had just like the devil
Stuck to that dead dog, bedevilled,
So himself he freely humbled.
That is why he's spared the killing.
But the leaves of his existence
Will but cease to turn in places,
When he is despised no longer.
Sneering masks concealing faces
Looked at him askance and priestly.
Zarathustra, calm and tranquil,
Passed them by, on to the forest
With the body of his neighbour,
Pacing o'er and o'er, retracing
In his heart of hearts the labour
Of the nations through the cycle
Of their days, he deeply pondered,
"They consider it much easier
Me to slay than those eternal,
Endless moments which had killed them

Long before their birthed existence,
By poor passions overpowering."
Seeing a house, he started knocking
On the door until an elder's
Voice awakened from its slumber.
"Who disturbs my sleep untimely?"—
"It is us, both dead and living.
Give us food and drink and lodging.
He who feeds by chance the hungry
His poor soul by chance refreshes."
Whereupon the elder vanished,
Then returned and brought his callers
Bread and wine for them to savour.
"Such an hungry place as this one
Is as good for habitation.
What is wrong with your companion,
Why will he not savour also?"
Asked the elder. Zarathustra
Answered, "Seems to me I hardly
Shall be able to persuade him
To consume the same way I do,
For he's dead now, as a dodo."
"Who the hell is he? I do not
Care that much for his existence.
Just one law of equal treatment —
Hospitality, I call it,
All deserve it, everybody.
Let him eat what I have offered."
Going farther on his pathway,
Zarathustra thought, reflecting

On the challenges of eating:
"Hungry places fit for living
That old man had simply chosen
For himself his self-disgraces
To conceal over the Cosmos
He had chosen as his birthplace.
That is why imprisoned travellers
By the Universe are nourished."
Zarathustra in the forest,
As he plunged into it deeper,
Found a hollow tree, enormous,
Placed therein his heavy burden,
Womb into a tomb converting,
Fell asleep and woke refreshened,
Found himself rejuvenated.
Then he scanned the well-known Planet,
Eyes agleam with sparkling trueness,
Skylark perched upon his shoulder,
"Now I need companions living
Who'd be able me to follow,
For it's harder with the dead ones:
Trained and trailed along behind me."

***

Autumn makes the leafy forest
Shed its yellow-reddish leafage,
Keeping warm the earth with heaven.
Tearful foliage falls until the
Skies are dry and weep no longer.

Truth, a new one, from a tablet
Newly-born now golden-tongued he
To his own dear heart was saying.
"Never more will I be speaking
To my daydreams, old and dead ones,
Withered well away, and wilted.
Now I need, indeed and truly,
At my home two homely hermits
With such delicate, fine hearing.
With my bliss I shall illumine,
With my joy, their hearts in heaven;
Songs will pour forth from my skylark,
Heart-felt songs, through revelation.
High-flying eagle will come save me,
Sapient serpent will assist me —
Soaring pride will take me higher,
Deeper sharp and eager wisdom;
Sunshine's smiling light enfolds them."

ZARATHUSTRA'S SONGS

Lark-like, I will sing the spirit ——
Fine-tuned ears are glad to hear it ——
His own role is self-amusing.
At the start his camel's nature
Of a sudden can compel his
Lack of wisdom to illumine
All things with delusive day-dreams,
Spirit satisfied, complacent.
He will now become enabled
At himself to laugh and others —
Yet in vain — old constellations.
It is good he is not rushing
For internal changes, Russian.
What will happen if inspired
Not by terror but by hatred
Of omniscient, powerful science?
Suddenly the spirit towers
Like a raging, violent lion
And his fear's replaced by boldness,
Clever, kind, audacious daring.
'I' for 'You' now substituted:
'You shall' into 'I will' altered.
But from where, then, does he gather
These lighthearted words "I'm soaring"? ——

Childish words to say is easy;
Hard to be like carefree children.
Spirit is the child creating,
On the wings of rising skylark,
A new art-like world in freedom
Where the Lion's had the teeth to
Brush away the Camel's stories.

***

Mountain air is pure and timid;
Spirits with resounding pinions
Fly around midst snow-white pinnacles.
Proud and dangerous my spirit,
Glad and soaring high in splendour,
As in lark-like elevation.
All of you look up with longing;
I gaze down, for I'm exalted.
Brave and bold, coercive slayers,
Value-breakers, soul-destroyers—
Our wise soul wants such creators.
You say life is just a boredom,
Difficult to bear and deal with.
That's your tenderness that covers
Your rebellious, shameless falsehood.
Harder for the rose to suffer
Fresh and trembling dewy waters.
You had better never tremble —
Wretched life accepts no weaklings.
You desire to live by habit —

So you think — in fact, by getting
Used to love which leaves you wounded.
Love, unskilled, hides drops of Spirit.
Pearled with dew, on rosebud petals
Sleep lies glazed with love, relaxing.
Butterflies display known pleasure,
Joy and happiness within them,
As the lark takes wing to azure
Sunlit skies with dew-pearled pinions
Tears of bliss gleam in my eyes, when
I observe these little spirits.
Seriousness will demonise you,
Slay you one after another.
Who's your father if your mother's
Nothing but your very other?
Barren wrath won't kill the demon;
Only your own sleepless laughter
Will possess him like a devil.

***

You aspire to exaltation,
Craving for the stars of spirit;
Foolishness has rushed for freedom
Like a dog, so wild and savage,
Staring up toward the heavens,
Barking angrily and crossly
From the doghouse, baying loudly
On a night the moon so tranquil.
They are prisoners of freedom

Whose sagacious, learned wisdom
Turns deceitful and dishonest.
Damp and dark the spirit's prison.
Cleanse the spirit and your eyes will
From their sleep awake, perceiving,
And with love and hope illumine,
Else your lofty elevation
Be disposed aspiring greatly
Towards both nobleness and meanness.
For the real and threatening danger's
Not in good but in destroying
Its divine shrine by your nature.
Vicious and pernicious poison
Fills your nature that destroys the
Skylark's height on which the blissful
Blessedness soars free in heaven.

***

Earth is rife with deadly preachers;
They preach death to all the nations.
You discern them by their faces
Inconspicuous, unassuming.
Welcome them as though convinced that
This our life goes on existing
After death —— of course, we're solaced.
From this life one must decoy them,
The superfluous, with this story.
They've no choice but being doomed to
Lacerate themselves, excited,

With a wish to die on exit,
And they mock their poor existence —
I will tell you — that last straw that
Holds them all by pleasant suffering.
They are frantic with great terror
At the moment their existence
Is horrendously uprooted.
It's the absence of death pleasant
That's most frighteningly appalling.
There's no providence in the falling
Of ascending lark from heaven.

*****

Most of all you dread mild mercy,
Being rendered gentle pity,
Spared by petty bores for Jesus:
It is mercy that's most dreadful.
I don't care to spare despisers,
Loathers of good-natured sparing
Lest they revel in their meanness.
The reward: when man's self-conquered
And his skylark has ascended.
Not your foes are all those loathed ones.
Petty friends can but demean you.
When you're heartless, then I love it,
Our chagrin at souls kind-hearted.
When you're loathsome, mean and ugly
Brace up not to be embarrassed.

23

***

See the sick, too eager monkeys
Striving for the heights of power,
Smelling foul from indigestion,
While devouring one another,
Worshipping their brand new idols:
Calling theft good education,
Newspapers — a black-bile vomit,
Priestly service — soul perversion.
Skylark's odes — a soma river
Fill your blood, intoxicating!

***

'Search for truth' you call your passion,
'Search for being' I call your anguish.
Do you want to conceive being? ——
Go to, then; it's quite a challenge
That requires it to become a
Meek reflection in the spirit.
Hear, O wise ones, this is nothing
But a lustful will to power;
Estimations of truth value
You will call your will triumphant,
As if rising like the skylark,
Adding your own will to the river
Of becoming, changing being.

***

Flee a woman's dream of passion;
Flee into the hands of killers —
If you don't, you'll die a woman.
Sorrow's filth-born as pure spirit:
Let what's called by everybody
Chastity, or virgin wisdom,
For the life of you, not touch you.
Not for meat it begs — red-bloody —
But for alms from poorest spirits.
Swine became the cast-out devil:
Do not cast it out or else you
Into swine will be converted.
Folly's to replace the devil.
Never asked, it paid a visit.
Woman hides both slave and tyrant,
Bright and dark together inside her,
And the man is full of nothing;
They are not a friend trustworthy;
But, as wills the lark ascending,
Be a friend unto your other.

***

You are noise-dazed by the great ones,
You'll be wasp-stung by the small ones.
Where your wilderness commences,
There you're caught in peaceful coldness.
Heart's blood — stiff in congelation.
And its wounds will soon be lead-filled;

While a devil's orchestration
Plays his visage seized with terror.
They will praise him as he plays at
Life and death — don't give to playing;
Just delve deep into your ego;
Rush into yourself, and quickly,
Ope your cage, set free your skylark.

ZARATHUSTRA IN TOWN

On the sky walked Zarathustra,
Following the skylark's skyway,
Heaven's cloth of clouds appearing
Smiling at the bridge and highway.
Like a hive the cripples round him
Hoped to get his thoughts by auction.
One of them, a sombre hunchback
Started speaking, him addressing,
"Just as waterfalls send splashes
Through the mounts, a whirlwind storm of
Thought within your name so rages,
Spreading diamond words on souls
With the fire of thought ignited,
Beast-like people thirst to hear the
Speeches destined all for goodness.
As a god we'll give you honour
Only if you heal our bodies."
Zarathustra spoke with healing,
"Look, O blind, upon the world-tide ——
You can see its secret deepness
In your heart of hearts, beholding
All creation's wondrous beauty.
You are happy in your daydreams.
Give I eyes to you, life's meanness

27

You shall see and in the sorrow
Of great suffering your soul will
Fall with inconsolable wailing,
And on earth you shall become one
Who's despairingly unhappy.
Look what role it has been playing,
That proud hunch in your existence:
You have learnt all expectations,
People's hopes for you and others,
With your mind so well developed
In profound, resounding feeling.
You are just a good-for-nothing
If you want to drop your virtue."
That dismayed the woeful hunchback,
"Yes, indeed you said this truly.
Why'd you say that all so bluntly?
You teach differently to others,
Like your reverent disciples."—
Whereupon the lark descended:
"Bunched-up ways are good with hunchbacks."

                    ***

Zarathustra makes a present —
As he leaves the crowded city
Called the "Motley Cow" by locals —
Of new consciousness to people:
"Gold's in many ways predestined
To be valuable and precious;
So intensely beam the values

28

Of unselfishness beloved.
Meek, illustrious the soft glance
Of the virtuous redeemer;
Sacrificial and unselfish,
The supreme glance of the giver.
To bestow himself he's ready.
For your goal's to stay forever
Spirit-breathing sacrifices,
Secret riches of the spirit
To accumulate and draw all
Things toward yourselves with vigour
So they'll flow again as presents.
Should your love commence by stealing
All your precious, dearest jewellery,
You shall name this fleeting moment,
Moment of a flitting skylark,
Selfishness so bright and holy.

***

Yet another selfishness, still
Poor and hungry and rapacious,
Prowls around just like a sick dog;
Unappeasable as ever
Is within its heart its hunger;
We feel terrified and say so:
Upward also goes our courseway,
Rising toward the supergenius.
Spirit buttresses the body
In endeavours, struggles, conquests.

If your heart among all others,
Full of life, a stream resembles,
Then your noble spirit wakens,
Rising from profound, deep slumber,
Like the lark, ascends in azure.
If your heart is like a river
Both a foul curse and a blessing
To its lowland banks, o'erflowing,
Then your will's at last discovered
The unique heart of a lover,
Early wit of thought and spirit —
Has decisively acquired.
Now the lark's secretive wing-beats
Of the stealthy, quiet morrow
Send to those with delicate hearing
The persistent blissful tidings:
As the radiant supergenius
With a brand new light approaches."

***

So reflected Zarathustra,
After that he simply added,
"As a lion hunts, unhurried,
As sail eagles high in heaven,
As the lark ascends in azure,
On my way I so continue
All alone, without companions.
On your way you, too, continue
All alone, without companions

And defend yourselves against me,
I may well have quite deceived you.
Do not learn to love your rivals,
Enemies and others only;
But proceed to learn to hate your
Very friends and good relations.
Pull my laurel wreath with vigour,
Tug at it as hard as can you,
For your awe for me will crush you,
Like a statue, hard collapsing,
Breaking into tiny pieces.
Find yourselves, with me abandoned,
As does Lark himself in azure;
Hear my parable in parting:

***

Zarathustra slept one morning,
Stealthily an adder slithered
To his side just as he covered
With his hand his face at dawning.
And the viper bit him, smiling.
Zarathustra scanned its eyes, then;
Evil eyes showing confusion.
'Thanks for waking me at morning' ——
He said kindly to the serpent,
'Please accept my thanks, and truly.
On ascending skylark's journey
I shall soon my way continue.'
But the snake in kind retorted:

31

'To turn up your toes, and sinew!'
'As a dragon I'm not frightened
By a commonplace snake's poison.
Do not waste your precious poison
For yourself and the poor planet.'
And the serpent lunged again, then,
To take back her own dear poison.
She turned out to be too willing
To restore his wound by licking."

ZARATHUSTRA'S RETURN

Parables are sown and planted
In the fertile soil of Spirit,
Sprouting forth with words and phrases,
Just like seeds, well germinating.
Zarathustra found his comfort
In the cavern's natural kingdom.
Many of his ideas ripen
Pressing on his brain, so painful,
Sprouting forth with force and vigour.
Meaning, joyfully maturing,
Ripens, too, and thirsts for giving,
And in no way for 'forgiving'.
Corn is glad to grow in number,
Striving to increase for people.
And his wisdom's grown in plenty
From the seed dropped by the skylark.
Suffering, pain, give seed to thinking.
Spirit's flames breathe more with freedom.
Zarathustra's sleep's disrupted
Suddenly by a seer-elder
Bringing in a lake-smooth mirror,
Smooth as silk in pitch-black darkness,
Saying, "Look, and you will surely
Recognise your very other."

Horror seizes Zarathustra ——
For he sees not quite his other,
But the devil with derision,
Staring back at him, and mocking.
He then wonders, "What a vision!
Can it carry any meaning?"
This is plainly the deduction:
It's a serious, grave corruption
Of the truth in my instruction.
Quite afraid of being uprooted,
Weeds and tares, both evidently,
Wished to pass as wheat, so hoping
To be spared from early judgement.
Enemies have just disfigured
Zarathustra in your spirit.
That is why I'm quickly losing
All my friends among all people."
Zarathustra leapt up, gleaming,
"I will keep my joyful madness:
And address my friends, enabled:
I've become a flowing river
That gives life a worthy meaning,
Waters rushing forth and breaking
Their new way into hearts of people.
I am a self-propelled creator ——
Lark propels himself to heaven:
By the old I'm tired of living.
Spirit wants no more the sneakers,
Old and worn-out, cheap and crappy.
Rushing to make my speech run faster,

I with joy leap into tempest,
Whip the wild steeds in my chariot.
I'm in love with those I talk to.
I am clouded with the tension
Of tempestuous, violent thunder,
Pour my thanks into your spirit.
My wild wisdom's now a mother:
She has just brought forth a baby:
Take him to your hearts now, people."

***

And the birch grove stands a wonder,
Lark beholding from up yonder:
Its green malachite seduces
With its gold's exquisite beauty;
And its yellow leafage tempts us
With its green and pleasant splendour;
And its whiteness wholly misses
Its grey sheen, so slim and slender.
Like a *skomorokh* there lies the
Mocking moss beneath the heavens ——
Like a toadstool there heaves its
Heavy breath to breathe for freedom.
Mushrooms are eclipsed by shadows
Cast by spider webs at evening;
Daylight is cut off, delightful,
By the lips' own ebb of sunlight.

***

Blowing north wind shakes the figs from
Slender trees: my tree-like wisdom
Will become a word trustworthy.
Sweet and ripe cascade the juices,
And the meat, so ripe and mellow,
Of the word of my tree-wisdom.
Peace is slowly made with noontide's
Hands between an earthy heaven
In the Fall of drowsy slumber
And a sentimental billow's
Sick, abominable weather.
From all suffering and sorrow,
Wrongs and ills you'll have tomorrow
Find your blissful liberation
In elation of creation.
Feelings pent, incarcerated
Suffer helplessly in prison ——
They will be the heavy hammer
That the hard stone block will shatter.
Of all images an image
Feelings see in their own other ——
Of delightful light the father:
As the lark keeps on ascending,
To the human race descending,
Good and evil now transcending
With his valuable acumen,
The resplendent *overhuman*!

***

Self-amused and blessed poets
Seek abused and blessed women,
Poor in dreaming, soft of skin, and
Write them poems on the billow,
Torturing their meagre spirit,
And their fragile flesh consuming.
Sewer ditches of decorum
Stirred by ripples show some deepness.
Isn't the billow a true peacock
Of true peacocks in this weather,
With its tail of fluffy feathers
Spread awry and gently sweeping
O'er the foamy, sandy beaches?
Spread so widely and so idly:
For it does not care to ponder
Who looks on to see it naked,
Maybe even a cow chewing
Cud in her protective cowshed
Or meandering through meadows.
What a nuisance is the billow,
An abominable bother!
They are hastening so quickly
To betake themselves out yonder.
Go and carry all your daydreams
High up to the fresh-air mountains,
Summon all your strength and bravely
Burn them one after another,
And disperse then their black ashes
Through the skylark's space of azure.

For I love this sea so angry,
Elemental in its nature,
Ready for dispute so heated:
It mysteriously harbours
Secretive and wavy women's
Own perpetual attraction.

***

An amazing skylark's azure
Marries curious words and phrases:
Leaves have strewn the ground with comfort,
Wind's performance acrobatic;
Moonlight's orchestra conducted;
Maestro grizzly graduated;
Nightingales licentious lechers;
Dry winds through the night-time rustling.
Fog has blanketed the berries,
Tasting the new dawn's illusion,
Draining from the dew its beauty,
Floats away, its paw still digging
In the heartland of the forest.

***

Nature's meadow streamed through bushes,
Winding on just like a river,
Midst intoxicated flowers.
Like gazelles, the playful maidens
Spun the drunk soul of the meadow.

"Dance, O maids," said Zarathustra.
"I am fond of a light spirit,
And will sing to you like skylarks:
I have looked into Life's azure
Eyes: they are beyond all measure,
Hard to penetrate and fathom."
Life replied with light derision,
"I'm so changeable a woman,
I am wild and void of virtue.
Men refer to me, as always,
As a mystery, enigma.
As is their prevailing custom,
With their virtue they endow me."
And she burst out laughing loudly
So one hardly could believe her.
As for me, I'm so distrustful
Of her speaking deep annoyance.
"Look right here," said flighty wisdom,
Of a sudden quickly melting.
"You embrace all of existence —
And on that account you praise it."
That excited me to anger
And to speak the truth to wisdom.
"Yes, I love life, yet I hate it
Even as I strongly love it.
Life is very much like wisdom —
So I'm fastened to existence."
Life enquired, "What's this wisdom?"
"Hard to catch, she's too elusive,
Fickle, bites her lip by habit,

39

Posing as a charming lady
Of dissemblance and deception."
Life guffawed at such an answer,
"Once again you're me describing?
Tell me all you know of wisdom!"
Life oped wide her eyes beloved,
I sank deep into their pupils.

***

In the night my soul's a fountain
Of larks' songs of fervent passion
That shoot straight to hearts, astounding.
Thirsty love to speak is longing:
Sucking light's full breasts with relish,
Wish I were as dark as darkness,
Then, my dear stars, I could bless you.
Scorched by my own flaming radiance,
I know not the gifts of gladness,
See my own light, no one else's.
From bright nights my thirsty envy
Does not rest: I see the sunlight.
By my heart's own gifts I'm sated ——
Hunger is the givers' sorrow.
I increase my hunger's beauty,
Wishing I could rob those gifted.
Plotting my revenge, I meanly
Give my tenderness with poison.

***

To the tombs of my youth yonder
I renounce my life eternal,
To my youthful love's own visions.
My dead visions stream with poison
To my heart, so sweet and tender.
I am affluent and lonely —
I who flower in remembrance
Of my virtuous and beloved.
Like a flock of birds so timid
You approached my eager longing,
Full of trust and expectations.
But the arrow of wild malice
Struck you hard and killed my birdies.
That is why my lark ascended.
My good foes, the curse against you:
You audaciously have taken
My eternity asunder,
And like phantoms you've assaulted.
Long ago my youth considered
All her days would be as holy.

***

Scornful monsters in derision,
Souls' sceptic apparitions
Crave the spirit's sublimation.
Seek your own spoil, not the hunter's.
In the forest of cognition
Spirits fought with beastly creatures,

Gazing out untamed and biting,
As a tiger jolly playful
With mankind and other species.
Let alone distinguished thinkers'
Own self-burdened sublimation,
Of their own sublimeness weary,
Casting off their self-deception,
Showing naked of good spirit.
A new morning starts with anguish,
Spirits self-surmount in whirling;
If they overleap their shadows,
As the lark takes wing from meadows,
They will reach the sun in twirling.

***

Laughter seized my fear of diverse
Pots' and paints' good-natured mother:
Faces dyed with tens of colours,
People looked so present daily.
There are very many mirrors
Round the world that nicely flattered.
Better masks, you will not find them ——
Likenesses are truer faces;
All masked peoples peep diversely
With their dreams and their traditions,
With their customs and religions.
In the underworld of shadows
The day-labourers —— much fatter
And much fuller than you living ——
I would rather see them daily.

42

All reality can do is make
Birds of passage shake all over.
Proud you are of your existence,
With beliefs absent entirely,
Though you've nothing to be proud of,
Pictures of your own perceptions
Which the lark transcends, ascending.
For reality must perish.

***

Lying moon, so broad and heavy,
Lay down in the throes of labour,
Set to bear a sun in daylight.
I do not believe that woman
But I would believe much sooner
There's a man on th'moon who wonders
Whether there's on earth a woman.
Woman is man's best worst healer.
All bad-conscienced men-night-dreamers
To a man bear small resemblance.
Like a cat upon a roof, one
Slinks by star-reflecting windows.
Men's feet tread so softly, gently,
As the moon with steps so furtive
Steals along by night till morning ——
No respect for them, dishonest.
This fine parable I offer
All insightful, pure discerners:
Shameful love and dirty conscience
Grip their minds like airy phantoms.

All earth-lovers are so moon-like,
One should call you lustful liars.
You deride the earthly strongly,
Though your bowels are much stronger
Than your good, decaying spirit
Which soothsays, "Without desiring
I behold the world, and not like
Craving dogs in heat of passion;
With my will already deadened,
Yet with still a happy conscience,
I'm through moon-like eyes perceiving
Planet Earth and all things purely.
I will lie before them as a
Genuinely reflecting mirror."
Lack of innocence of desiring
Makes you all the more blameworthy:
You defile all your desiring.
Hypocrites, voluptuous, lustful,
Your divine skin has enshrouded
Teeming snakes with their bad odour.
Dare believe your very other,
First of all, your very bowels.
Thirst's desire divinely rises,
From the billow's depths ascending
To the lark's domain of azure;
Wanting to be kissed by sunshine.
Like the sun, I love existence:
Life does not exhaust its deepness,
Like the lark I sing my praises
To myself whom life embraces.

***

Just like cows, long-hornèd mountains
Pierce the dark cloud's bushy eyebrows:
Red blood drips from sunset's glowing;
Whale-like islands lying scattered,
Their volcano for a giant
Volatile, mad spout's sore breathing.
As the vessel tilts and tosses,
People watch a shadow flying
Straight for the fire-spitting crater.
Zarathustra's flighty shadow
Floated right inside the bowels
Of the Earth now in broad daylight.
People curiously wondered:
"Looks as if the devil took him."
"Not at all!" someone responded,
As if Lark through one had spoken —
"Looks as if he took the devil."

***

Dark clouds are the shawl of twilight;
Bright clouds are the veil of sunlight;
Rainbows are the girdle of heaven.
Skylarks are the Earth's ascensions.
With long moles' flat tongues, the breakers
Lapped at the shoals wide and shallow,
With the teeth of cliffs now foaming;
Billows moaning, rolling over,
Seagulls shrieking in the dawning.

THE QUIET HOUR

What has happened? What has happened?
I'm to leave you of a sudden,
But the bear is most unwilling
Back to its own lair to lumber,
Lacking courage to forsake you,
And the skylark's not descending.
What strange genius calls upon me?
It's the god of all my moments ——
Called 'The Quiet Hour' humbly.
In the pleasant evening's silence
He came on to argue with me,
And the ground just sank beneath me.
Blessing sleep, then, took me over.
I was frightened by the stillness,
Yet the Quiet Hour was speaking,
As if whispering, or voiceless,
"Well you know it, Zarathustra,
But you dare not e'en admit it
To yourself, so fearful, feeble."
I cried out just like a baby:
"It is true I cannot do it?"
But the voice again responded,
"What is that to you? Come on, just

Break and say your own confession." —
"I await the worthier other."
"You've received as yet no blessing." —
"At the foothills of my mountain
I reside and no one's told me
What you have." I answered, crying,
"And although I talked to people,
Still my vibrant speeches drifted
By and caught no one's attention."
"He who's able to move mountains,
Well can move low lands and valleys.
Quiet words, you should remember,
Can bring on a stormy tempest.
Your own fate you shall foreshadow:
Thoughts that tread with doves' soft footsteps
Guide the present world in secret."
"I'm ashamed," I said. His laughter
Pained my heart, excruciating,
"When a child, you'll drop such shyness.
Youth through pride retards your progress.
You'll appear unripe before your
Fruitful offspring if you do not
Leave your youth, becoming child-like."

***

From dark forests autumn's twilight
Sends the lark a nightfall warning.
Lark descends with oozing sunlight
Peacefully to rest till morning.

Neath the stone the serpent settles,
To his lair the bear now lumbers,
In his nest the eagle nestles,
In his den the lion slumbers.

Now the russet cow of sunset
Rushes over the horizon ––
Of a silent night the onset ––
With a night-time life surprising:

Night is born and evening dying,
Lying moon is up and spying,
Twinkling stars the Earth is eyeing,
Silent breeze is softly sighing.

Nature's morning soon awakens:
And the scarlet calf arising
With the dawn, with joy o'ertaken,
Scurries high from the horizon.

Little cubs wake bear and lion,
Hatchling sees an eaglet flying,
Lark ascends to heaven, skying ––
All can hear a new-born crying.

www.ingramcontent.com/pod-product-compliance
Lightning Source LLC
Chambersburg PA
CBHW071742020426
42331CB00008B/2136